A tree has many parts.

leaves

branches

trunk

roots

Many plants and animals make their homes in the different parts of a tree.

scarlet tanager

gray treefrog

chipmunk

gypsy moth
caterpillar

red flat bark beetle

ant

fungus

In the highest branches, a mother bird feeds her babies an insect she has found nearby.

And an owl rests before a long night of hunting.

In its nest at the top of a tree, a baby squirrel waits for its mother to return.

Nearby, a hungry porcupine eats its favorite foods—the tree's buds, twigs, and bark.

The woodpecker makes holes in the bark of the tree's trunk, looking to eat the insects that make their home there.

A hole in the trunk is a perfect place for bees to make their nest,

and for a raccoon, too!

The rough bark of the lower trunk is a place where vines and fungi sometimes grow.

The bottom of the tree is a nice spot for a little animal, like this deer mouse, to make its nest.

This red fox is safe and warm in the home it has dug around the tree's roots.

The cicada nymph burrows in the soil around the tree's roots, waiting to become an adult.

The earthworm helps to keep soil healthy for trees and other plants.

On the ground,
a squirrel looks
for acorns,

and a deer munches on bark and leaves from the branches above.

Did you think you would find so much life in a tree?